• HALSGROVE DISCOVER SERIES ➤

BURY ST EDMUNDS

Alan Childs

With maps by Ashley Sampson

HALSGROVE

To Sue, John and Lesley
With Love

First published in Great Britain in 2014
Copyright © Alan Childs 2014

British Library Cataloguing-in-Publication Data
A CIP record for this title is available from the British Library

ISBN 978 0 85704 033 6

HALSGROVE
Halsgrove House,
Ryelands Business Park,
Bagley Road, Wellington, Somerset TA21 9PZ
Tel: 01823 653777   Fax: 01823 216796
email: sales@halsgrove.com

Part of the Halsgrove group of companies
Information on all Halsgrove titles is available at:
www.halsgrove.com

Printed in China by Everbest Printing Co Ltd

Acknowledgements and sincere thanks to the following individuals and bodies

Mike Ames; Angel Hotel; Tony Appleton; Athenaeum staff; Elizabeth Barber-Lomax; Brown and Scarlett; Jack Burton; Bury St Edmunds' Library staff; Bury St Edmunds' Town Council; Suffolk Record Office; Nick Clarke; Bruce Elliot; Jean Evans; Liz and Tony Fayers; Sarah Friswell (Cathedral staff); Guildhall Feoffment Community Primary School (Mrs S.C. Herriott); Susan Hindry; Jen Larner; Don MacKenzie; Alex McWhirter; Methodist Church (Revd. V. Spencer); Moyse's Hall staff; Nutshell Public House; Jean Pickering; St Edmundsbury Borough Council; St John's Church; St Mary's Church; Neil Storey; Theatre Royal (Lucy Close); Sam Thompson; Bury Tourist Information Centre; Unitarian Church; Nicola Warton; Mark Woods.

I am particularly grateful to the following proof readers/local experts: Mike Ames BEM; Sarah Childs; Brian Coley; Peter Minter; Geoff Storey; Sue Wharfe and Lesley Yeldham.

To my two good friends, Ashley Sampson, and Ron Wiebe, I am enormously grateful. Their multitude of skills, especially in computers, has guided me along untrodden paths. Ashley in addition, is an experienced cartographer and has masterminded the use of the 1886 First Edition Ordnance Survey 25 inch maps of Bury. Kate Vaughan at the Record Office has also been of tremendous help.

I acknowledge with many thanks the loan of the following material: Athenaeum staff; photos of the Theatre Royal, Bury St Edmunds (National Trust photographer Dennis Gilbert); photos from the Cathedral collection (Dean and Chapter); the kind permission of the St Edmundsbury Borough Council Heritage Services to photograph inside Moyse's Hall.

My thanks also to Simon Butler and Sharon O'Inn for all help and support from Halsgrove.

Finally, in addition to a number of excellent books on the history of Bury St Edmunds to which I have turned (eg the work of Frank Meeres and Margaret Statham), I should like especially to acknowledge as sources, firstly the writings of the late Alec Clifton-Taylor, an architectural historian of great gifts, and secondly, that guru of all things architectural, the late Nikolaus Pevsner, ('Suffolk' in 'The Buildings of England' series).

Author's Note

IN THE EARLY 1970s I worked in the village of Brettenham and visited Bury St Edmunds on my days off. I got to know and love the town, and enjoyed the richness of its architectural heritage. I was also doing research into the history of Suffolk elections of former years, largely at the Bury Record Office, and there encountered the fictional borough of 'Eatanswill' for the first time. Dickens did not of course base this 'rotten borough' upon Bury, but another Suffolk town!

'Bury St Edmunds' includes five walking routes and a sixth car route to allow readers to explore Bury St Edmunds using the book. As a background to these walks it has been possible to make use of the delightful 1886 Ordnance Survey 25 inch map, in its first (coloured) edition. The routes have been superimposed upon a not so different Victorian street plan which provides added interest in the 19th century details found there. Walks can be started at any entry point and are linked, for convenience.

It is in the nature of such projects as this that it is impossible to approach all who may appear in a general photograph, particularly when the final list is a long way off. Similarly, when including buildings, it is impossible to approach all owners. The photographs have of course been taken from 'public places' where anyone could stand to view or photograph, so I trust, in this sense they are not intrusive. I naturally hope that their inclusion here will give pleasure, and together with the text, will be of interest to all who love the town. By virtue of Bury's riches, it has been a case of fitting a quart into the proverbial pint pot, so it is very much a personal selection - others would have done it differently. I also hope that I may be forgiven by native 'Burians' in as much as the book has originated from a 'foreigner' - from over the county boundary!

Alan Childs
Sheringham, Norfolk.

Introduction

THE HISTORY OF Bury St Edmunds, formerly Bedricesworth, is a long and honorable one, that of a provincial town of stature, whose own local history has frequently impinged upon national affairs. Its motto 'Sacrarium Regis, Cunabula Legis' means 'Shrine of the King, Cradle of the Law'. Interestingly, in its subsequent name, the word 'Bury' is connected with 'Burgh', a fortified town, rather than burial. 'Kings and princes offered great gifts at the shrine of St Edmund, third in importance after Canterbury and Walsingham. King Canute was responsible for founding the Benedictine monastery; Edward the Confessor visited the Abbey and bestowed privileges upon it, including the right to mint coins; William the Conqueror added further privileges and increased the number of monks; Richard I gave thanks there for his safe return from imprisonment during the Third Crusade'. King John also visited Bury, somewhat ironically perhaps if the story of the preliminary Bury St Edmunds' meeting of the barons with Archbishop Stephen Langton, in November 1214, is a true one. The source of this story is Roger of Wendover, a monk of St Albans.

In William's great Domesday Book of 1086, - the first group of bureaucrats, with forms to be filled in about the personal details of the poor old Saxons - Bury was guessed to have a population of 4,000 (F.M.), double that of the Conquest year of 1066. It was a substantial settlement and few like-towns could boast a mint, or the honour of Parliament being convened within their walls.

Throughout the centuries of its history the power of the abbey was enormous and the very shape of the town today, with its grid-pattern streets, is the result of the planning of Baldwin, one of its early abbots. He was a remarkable man, able to turn his hand to a myriad of tasks. Baldwin had formerly been Edward the Confessor's court physician, and was also William the First's.

The story of Edmund himself and the impact the saint seemed to have had, both before but also after his martyrdom, is a fascinating one and full of mystery. The basic facts are as follows:

King Edmund was the last king of East Anglia. Rather surprisingly he had been offered the throne by King Offa of East Anglia who was apparently impressed by the young man when Offa visited Saxony, of which kingdom Edmund's father was king. On the sudden death of Offa, Edmund was invited to England to take up his throne. He landed, tradition has it, at Hunstanton in Norfolk, in 855. He was crowned at Christmas the following year and went on to rule his people well.

A serious Danish invasion took place and King Edmund fought against the invaders. The Anglo Saxon Chronicle describes what happened:

'In this year (869/70) the army rode over Mercia into East Anglia, and took winter quarters at Thetford; and in that winter King Edmund fought against them, and the Danes gained the victory, and slew the king, and subdued all that land.' Edmund had been captured and when he refused to renounce his faith, was shot to death by arrows, and his body decapitated. Legend has it that a wolf guarded his head and when his followers were searching, the head apparently called out 'Here, Here, Here', to guide them. It was Edmund's death that led directly to the building of the Abbey in Bury, to provide a fitting resting place for the mortal remains of the king. In 903 his body was brought from Sutton to the then Bedricesworth. The Abbey was to become one of the foremost in the country, and its presence affected much of Bury's future development.

The riches of Bury's buildings and architecture are astonishing, almost 1,000 listed (or similar) buildings; round every corner are delightful houses and fascinating architectural details. Moyse's Hall, for example, now a museum, has had many roles in its long history, dating from Norman times. It is a rare domestic survivor from that time. The Georgian period, however, is of course generously represented. Local East Anglian (mainly Suffolk and Essex) specialities include 'pargeting'. Sometimes appearances can be deceptive however, particularly where buildings are concerned. Scratch the apparent Georgian exterior and a much older timber-framed building may lie beneath. It was of course the timber-framing, as in so many towns that contributed to the disastrous fire of 1608. If London a few decades later was to lose so much, it is not surprising that Bury suffered likewise. Fire-fighting methods were primitive with hooks to pull down burning thatch and gunpowder to create a fire-break. 'Insurance' was stringent and without the right fire badge the firefighters would not visit! One such badge is still displayed here. The Bury fire is blamed on the negligence of a servant in an Eastgate Malt House.

The flames spread from Looms Lane into the market place. It destroyed an estimated 160 houses, with twice that number of outbuildings and 'houses of necessary use'.

Bury is nevertheless fortunate in retaining many of its original shop-fronts, delightful to look at, even if maintenance is far harder. The town also has a truly magnificent open space in Angel Hill, (formerly the 'Mustowe', or meeting place) surrounded by a time line of old buildings and originally the scene of Bury's ancient charter fair, each autumn. The fair was granted in 1272 and lasted some 600 years until rowdyism caused its demise. As was usual at fairs, summary justice was dispensed at the court of 'Pie Powder' (pied poudre, meaning dusty feet). It was one of three fairs in Bury's history. Henry III was reputed to have sent his tailor to Bury Fair for Flemish fur robes. Bury was a wool-manufacturing town and its wool was 'fulled' and its yarn was sold, while cloth and clothing were frequently imported. In later year Henry VIII's sister Mary Tudor often visited the fair.

In the Middle Ages craft guilds were an important feature of the life of a town. Bury had 17 guilds at various times. The Bakers were the earliest, and the list included the Cordwainers (workers in leather) and the Linen and Woollen Weavers. Guilds were often involved in local entertainments, and research seems to indicate that a version of the Medieval mystery plays was found here.

Bury has in Greene King its own long-established and very successful brewery, following the monastic example of producing good Suffolk beer. Close-by their brewery is a gem of a Regency theatre, leased now to the National Trust. It has survived intact, despite being used as a brewery barrel store for a time! There is a railway station whose two towers could well have originated in Venice. The town also had, during its medieval history, six hospitals, but using the word in its medieval sense of 'almshouse', where the poor were tended. As was common, the hospitals were situated near the town gates. Some distance from the town centre, along Eastgate, is to be found the remaining window of one such

A dove-cote is included in the original Abbey buildings.

hospital, the leper hospital of St Petronilla, placed in a new position. In Northgate Street, Bury can claim the honour of having the Gage family residence, the family from Hengrave Hall who introduced greengages to England. The town's two rivers are delightfully named the Lark and the Linnet and, as is to be expected, the street names and such like are themselves redolent with history: Bridewell Lane and Butter Market; Brentgovel Street and Looms Lane; Out Risbygate and Honey Hill.

East Anglia, with its flatter landscape was the home of numerous air-fields during World War Two, and Bury had its own station at Rougham. The close presence of the American 94th Bombardment Group, equipped with the Boeing B17s, the legendary 'Flying Fortresses', is reflected in the tribute rose garden in the Abbey grounds. Bury suffered earlier from Zeppelin attacks in the First World War.

Over the years, the good and the great have visited Bury St Edmunds, or stayed within its walls: Queen Elizabeth I visited as part of her Suffolk 'progress'. Charles Dickens enjoyed the hospitality of the 'Angel', when giving his dramatic readings in Bury, as did Samuel Pickwick. The novelist Maria Louise Rame ('Ouida') was born in Bury St Edmunds. Edward Fitzgerald went to school here and Oscar Wilde visited to lecture. John Wesley preached in a small building in St Mary's Square where Thomas Clarkson, the anti-slave-trade campaigner also had a house (1806-16) having married Catherine Buck, of Bury. They were friends of William and Dorothy Wordsworth and the latter stayed with them here. Daniel Defoe stayed in Abbeygate Street and found the town 'most thronged with gentry'. The composer Liszt performed in the Concert Room of the Market Cross, a building designed by Robert Adam. Humphrey Repton was born here, as was the theatre director Sir Peter Hall and also Bob Hoskins. John Le Mesurier lived locally and Ian McShane ('Lovejoy') was given the freedom of the Borough! Norah Lofts wrote her popular novels in the charming Northgate House.

William Cobbett in his 'Rural Rides' of 1830 was effusive and almost embarrassingly complimentary about the town:
'To conclude an account of Suffolk and not to sing the praise of Bury St Edmunds would affront every creature of Suffolk birth: even at Ipswich, when I was praising that place, the very people of that town asked me if I did not think Bury St Edmunds the nicest town in the world'!

Today Bury St Edmunds is a town of more than 35,000 inhabitants, with the 4th oldest non-league football club in Britain, founded way back in 1872, playing at Ram Meadow Stadium. It was also one of 11 founding members of the Suffolk County FA, thirteen years later.

Most importantly, there is a watchful town council and a vigilant 'Bury St Edmunds Society' - a group of people rightly dedicated to the protection of their town. Its formation came about in 1971, when a plan to demolish large areas of 'Brackland', including the atmospheric St John's Street, was put forward. The stated aim of the Society is:
'To ensure that, whilst Bury St Edmunds continues to grow and prosper, it remains a beautiful town in which to live, work or visit.' The town's heritage must be preserved, but equally, modern developments must sometimes be countenanced, after due (and often heated) debate. Each century will make its mark on any historical town, even if difficult to accept at the time, and none can be wrapped in moth-balls. The buildings are part of a living and lively community, so changes will come about. But Bury St Edmunds is a town that wears its history well. The story is there beneath its stones and bricks and timbers for anyone willing to dig below the surface. It is a fascinating story and Burians are justly proud of their much-praised town.

The Bury St Edmunds Town Council was granted the Royal Licence to use the Arms and Crest in 2006. In the colourful Norman French of heraldry the coat of arms is described as follows (the modern equivalent of some of the words is shown in square brackets):

Azure [blue, the background colour] three Coronets Or [gold] each enfiled by a pair of Arrows saltire-wise [crossed diagonally] points downwards, Argent [silver]. Crest: Upon a helm with a Wreath Or [gold] and Azure [blue] a Wolf sejany [sitting on haunches] proper [in natural colour] holding a King's Head couped [severed] also proper [in natural colours] crowned Or [gold]. Mantled [fronds of fabric falling from below the wreath and draped on each side of the Helm] Gules [red] doubled [mantling turned back to reveal some of the reverse side] Argent [silver].

The motto in Latin is: Sacrarium regis, cunabula legis [shrine of the king, cradle of the law]. This refers to the burial of King Edmund here, and the story (not entirely substantiated) of the meeting of the Barons at Bury Abbey in 1214, preceding Magna Carta. This emphasises the historic importance of Bury St Edmunds. [Our grateful thanks to the Town Council for permission to use their coat of arms.]

The stone equivalent is to be seen above the former Borough Council Offices on Angel Hill.

Tucked away at the back of the cathedral, just off Angel Hill, is this delightful mosaic. Some time back there was a focus on 'greening' the cathedral and a competition was run on this theme, using the mosaic art-form. Revd. Selwyn Swift was the winner. His entry showed all sorts of 'green' additions to the cathedral, including wind turbines and rainwater harvesters. The design was turned into a mosaic by Rojo Art, but the work to put it together was by visitors to the Suffolk Show of that year.

Opposite: The plaque reads: 'This cast aluminium sculpture by Jonathan Clarke was created as a vision of hope, and speaks of pilgrimage and journey. By coincidence, 'Godspeed' was the name of the ship in which Bartholomew Gosnold, one of the earliest explorers of New England, set sail. Gosnold, who worshipped at this church (St James's), named Martha's Vineyard after his infant daughter who died, and was buried in Bury St Edmund's Great Churchyard. He also named Cape Cod. Jamestown in Virginia, was also one of the first New England settlements and named by Gosnold. It could be claimed that by doing this he prevented the embryonic nation from being claimed by Spain.

Godspeed V.

In our modern era it is rare for the citizens of a town to witness, and be a part of, the growth of a beautiful cathedral. In former centuries generations of worshippers and skilled craftsmen were involved in such massive building projects and the time-scale for construction was in many cases an enormous one. Abbot Anselm (1121-48) had been responsible for the original church on which the Cathedral is today based; it was first dedicated to St Denis but later to St James, in honour of another St James in Compostella, whose shrine Anselm had hoped to visit. Although Bury's second St James's church (mainly constructed 1503-1551) was not complete when Henry VIII wielded his axe on the monasteries, his son, Edward VI, somewhat ironically, contributed £200 towards its completion. John Wasbell was one of the Master Masons involved with building the Cathedral and Simon Clerk was also involved. It was as late as 1914 that a new diocese of 'St Edmundsbury and Ipswich' was created. The act of Parliament necessary for this, raised the status of this former parish church to that of 'Cathedral Church'.

13

Cathedrals have never been static monuments; they are indeed buildings that evolve and grow. This was never more true than when Bury St Edmund's skyline changed dramatically with the addition of the 150ft. 'Lantern Tower'. This Millennium-inspired tower was constructed between 2000-2005 and was designed by Hugh Mathews. Traditional skills were used, with materials to blend sympathetically: Barnack limestone, flint and lime mortar. Examples of a technique called 'flushwork' can be seen on the tower, where the 'knapped' flint and limestone are set 'flush' with each other, to form a contrasting pattern of light and dark materials.

A building for all seasons

God blessed them saying multiply

God created man in his own image

This shows part of the 'Creation Window', in the west wall of the north aisle, by Clayton and Bell. It is the story of God's creation of the world in seven days. It was given in memory of John Wollaston Greene (1869-1925), who was the first registrar of the diocese of St Edmundsbury and Ipswich, from its foundation in 1914 until he died.

God planted a garden in Eden   God said I will make him an help meet

Several decades later, in 1960, the eminent architect Stephen Dykes Bower (1903-1994) was invited to assist in the church's enlargement and development. Dykes Bower was a 'Gothic Revival' architect, known for his work at Westminster Abbey and St Paul's. At Bury St Edmunds he was responsible for the rebuilding of the chancel, plus the transepts and side chapels. Stephen Dykes Bower obviously had an eye for 'recycling! Amazingly he used heating grills from a redundant church in Manchester to create beautiful screens and gates (the work by E. Furneaux and Son, of Bishops Stortford). His chandeliers are also beautiful in their simplicity.

The substantial funding needed for the tower was raised partly from the Millennium Commission, partly from a most generous £2 million legacy in the will of Stephen Dykes Bower but partly also from Suffolk individuals, who raided their savings to support this once-in-a-lifetime appeal. Prince Charles was an enthusiastic supporter of the project. A new Chapel of the Configuration and the Cloisters were completed in 2008.

Opposite: The ceiling of the new tower had its 'topping- out' ceremony in January 2010. It is a spectacular coloured and gilded oak ceiling, made up of more than 3,000 parts. The project manager was Horry (sic) Parsons and the 'implementing architect', Henry Freeland.

This owl and the pussy cat look much too contented to go to sea! Could it be that he is the cathedral cat, watching over the precinct. He was observed near-by St James's and was certainly streetwise and unbothered by humans. There was scarcely a glance as the camera drew closer. The owl was equally unconcerned and would sit on the pole for ever it seems, without moving.

Regarding ornaments, not everything is hidden away in the back gardens. Owners sometimes delight in amusing additions to the 'public side' of their properties and give the passers-by some fun as well.

The impressive space that is Angel Hill, plays host to numerous events, including of course its annual fairs. It is the heart of Bury St Edmunds.

The 'Norman Tower' was built between 1120 and 1148 by Abbot Anselm, as a gate to the Abbey Church. It is a fine example of its period, The side it shows the town is a little more ornate. And the arch is somewhat porch-like. It is sometimes called 'Church Gate', or 'St James's Gate'. By the Tudor period it was acting as the bell tower, or 'campanile', for the nearby St James's Church, and contains a peal now of 12 bells (increased from 10). The interesting Norman detail includes inter-secting arches. Its original battlements were lost in the 19th century and the amusing gargoyles are additions from that time. The limestone for its construction originated in the Barnack quarry, following an arrangement with the monks of Peterborough. The transport, in flat-bottomed boats, was an enormous task. William the Conqueror pulled royal 'rank' in ordering the Abbot of Petersburgh to allow Burg Abbey to take Barneck Stone.

Dame Elisabeth Frink (1930-93) was best known for her bronze outdoor sculptures and was a very busy sculptress with many commissions. Her modern interpretation of St Edmund, with hints of Crusader style, was commissioned by the former West Suffolk County Council, when it was merged with East Suffolk in 1974 to become the Suffolk County Council. Although the statue was originally intended for the town centre, the present site is surely a most appropriate one.

The relationship of the Abbey to the town was often a stormy one, and things bubbled to a head in the summer of 1327. The townspeople's wrath at constant impositions was vented on the Great Gate to the Abbey, which they destroyed. The gate we see today with its fine ornamentation and detail, is the subsequent re-building, completed around 1353. In its heyday this gate was the 'business' access to the Abbey. Today it is most visitors' entry to the Abbey Gardens, through what was originally the 'Great Court'.

The Rule of the Abbey was that of St Benedict of Nursia, the first community being that at Monte Cassino in Italy. Monks shared the domestic chores, and had the pleasure of a 2 a.m. start in the summer. In England, Bury Abbey would certainly earn its place in the leading six Benedictine religious communities. With our perspective of many centuries it is hard to appreciate the sheer magnificence of Bury St Edmund's Abbey. It was a microcosm of a city, with so many individual parts to appreciate. Its scale was unbelievable, as the often reproduced 'reconstruction' in the painting by W.K. Hardy (1880) shows. The Norman Tower led straight across to the enormous West Front, whose substantial arches have now been in-filled by domestic buildings. The nave stretched 50 ft. further than that of Norwich Cathedral and the Western Tower was gigantic. How difficult it is today, even for adults, to gain anything of an understanding from the sporadic clumps of stonework that mark the boundaries of this enormous collection of buildings. As Pevsner commented: 'What remains of it now are two mighty gates into the Precinct, and inside it, no more than fragments which tell their tale only to the student'. His estimate of its size was 1500 ft. from N to S and about 1000 ft. from W to E.

A Tudor visitor, John Leland, writing in 1534, was greatly impressed by the scale of Bury Abbey:

'A man who saw the Abbey would say verily it were a city, so many gates there are in it, and some of brass: so many towers and a most stately church, upon which attend three other churches, also standing gloriously in the same churchyard, all of passing fine and curious workmanship.'

A non-comprehensive list of its component parts would include: Abbot's bakery and brewery; Abbot's hall over the cellar; Abbot's stable; bakery; bath; Black Hostry; brewery; buttery (wine not butter!); cowshed; dovecote; granary; Great Hall over the cellar; infirmary; inner parlour; kitchen; lecture court; mill; Queen's chamber over the larder and wardrobe; school; song school;

treasury; warming house; watermill et cetera, et cetera, et cetera. A plan by A.J. Whittingham contains over 80 identifiable parts. It was vast! In addition to this, the Abbey owned virtually every building in the town that had grown up around it. It was immensely rich and also owned the so-called 'Liberty of St Edmund', granted by the Confessor. This was comparable in area to the former West Suffolk. With its religious pedigree and the 'miracles' that were claimed at St Edmund's shrine, it attracted pilgrims from all over the world. As a pilgrimage centre in this country, it was third only to Canterbury and Walsingham.

Graduation is a high point in young students' lives and how better to celebrate this special day in the surroundings of the abbey and cathedral. Throughout the year the cathedral offers a wonderful venue for such events as does the background of the abbey gardens.

When cemetery space became limited, recourse to a charnel house was often necessary, as here at Bury. It was simply an additional and economical storage of ancient bones. Bury's Chapel of the Charnel dates from the c.1300 and in its history has done service as an inn and a blacksmith's premises! It was sold as a private mausoleum.

Below: This fine house within the precincts of the former abbey was built in 1730 as the Clopton Asylum. Dr Poley Clopton died in 1730 and, in his will, endowed a charity to establish an almshouse or asylum for 12 poor men and 12 women of the parishes of St James and St Mary. Dr Clopton endowed the charity with lands in Foxearth, Stisted and Braintree. The Clopton Trustees purchased the land in 1735 and the first residents arrived in 1744. The Clopton coat of arms is over the centre of the building. Its later function for the building is as 'The Provost's House' of the cathedral.

The ups and downs of the former abbey's terrain are exciting for children to explore and a paradise for students of our monastic heritage. For the general public the interpretation of these former buildings is not perhaps easy, but the batteries are recharged and the 'abbeyscape' is a very special place.

What remains today is the most amazing series of gardens and open spaces of incomparable value to the town. In 1806 the Bristol family inherited the gardens, but it was under William IV that the landscaping of the Abbey Gardens began, modelled on Brussels' Royal Botanical Gardens. Bury's gardens were opened originally in 1831 as 'Subscription Gardens' with unlimited access for the sum of two guineas a year! Towards the end of the 19th century the general public was allowed in at one shilling for adults and sixpence for children. In 1912 the gardens were leased by the Borough Council from the Bristol family and were then made freely available. The original gardens were laid out by Nathaniel Hodgson and the Borough Council purchased them in 1853.

These immaculate gardens are tended by a staff of about five. Throughout the year there are floral masterpieces to lift the spirits, from the first snowdrops and aconites. Very tame squirrels stalk generous human-beings. Through summer, there are delightful displays in the rose gardens. The park is a 'green lung' for Bury and its area, suiting every purpose, from the casual stroller or naturalist, to the doers or watchers of crowd-pulling happenings and entertainments. Two particular points of interest in the gardens are the Memorial Rose Garden, in tribute to the USAF servicemen (especially the 94th Bombardment Group) who

lost their lives in World War II. The seat in the same area is shaped from the wing of a B17 ('Flying Fortress'). In another area there is a reconstructed herb garden commemorating Abbot Baldwin.

When in 1539 the monasteries were felled, for a tangled mixture of Henry VIII's motives, it was soon as if they had not existed. At Bury the lead was stripped from the Abbey's roofs and the stonework underwent a rapid Tudor recycling, occasionally speeded up by gunpowder! The weather was thus allowed in and the decay was rapid. It was said to have been sold for £413.

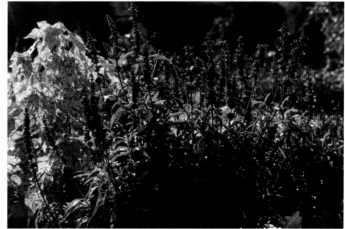

It is likely that one of John Wesley's preachers visited Bury in 1754 and Wesley himself came the following year. In all he visited Bury seventeen times. In his day 5 a.m. services were not unusual. In 1812 the first Weslyan church was opened in St Mary's Square on the site of a house owned by the Jewers sisters. With the growth of 'Primitive' Methodism, an alternative chapel was established here in 1830. The Weslyan 'New Trinity Chapel' the main chapel today, was opened in March 1878, 270 people taking tea in the schoolroom. The Weslyans became involved in education and the Primitive Methodists (moving to bigger premises on the corner of Looms Lane) with the agricultural labourers. 1932 saw the beginning of the coming together and the Primitive Methodist chapel was sold soon afterwards.

The years following the Reformation were extremely difficult ones for those who remained within the Roman Catholic fold. Their civil rights were eroded and they were made criminals. It was an act of treason to house a Catholic priest and larger houses had 'priest's holes' to secure their safety. There were hidden 'mass centres' locally, at Lawshall, Long Melford and Hengrave Hall. In 1633 Jesuit priests established the 'College of the Holy Apostles' in Bury, followed by a school in part of the former abbey. This was attacked by a mob in 1688 and the priests fled. They returned however, and by 1762 a priest's house and a chapel, now the Blessed Sacrament chapel, were built on the present site. The anti-Catholic laws were abolished in 1829 leading to the present church of St Edmund being built in 1837. Schools followed, beginning with an elementary school in 1882 (now St Edmund's Primary School). The present St Benedict's secondary school was opened in 1967. Today's church, the oldest post-Reformation church in use in the diocese, was designed by Charles Day. Inside, pieces of an 18th century marble fireplace from Rushbrooke Hall have been incorporated and two large door-cases framing the altar are also from this hall. The box pews are from the original church as are the pulpit and altar rails.

It seems generous when a household shares the interior details of its home with passing strangers! Decorated windows can be a delight. Some people have taken a good deal of trouble with their displays but two or three carefully-chosen objects can work equally well. Bury has a few examples of 'Venetian' windows to look out for. In architectural terms, they are the three-sectioned windows with a central arch, so characteristic of the 16th to 18th centuries' 'Palladian' style. Reputedly the Venetian window was first used in Britain by Inigo Jones.

There is no need to journey to Dublin or Edinburgh New Town to see fine door-cases, so typical of the Georgian period. Bury St Edmunds has originals in abundance, of every colour and design. The fanlights - the rectangular or semi-circular window above the door, lighting the hallway - are intriguing in their variety. The doors of this period often have additional details or 'furniture' such as knockers and hinges, letter-boxes and locks, boot-scrapers and name plates. Crown Street and Hatter Street are but two examples of many streets with Georgian doors throughout the town.

The word jettying is used to describe the way in which a timber-framed house seems to get wider as the house gets taller. Sometimes the 'overhang' (it can be as much as four feet) is just on one or two sides, but occasionally it is all the way round. It is a feature much seen across the country and, as in Bury or Lavenham, even where stucco (plaster) has been applied, the evidence of an overhang betrays the timber-framing. So a house could be much older than at first glance.

One of the intriguing things is that, despite the widespread use of jettying in the Middle Ages and Tudor periods, there is no clear-cut answer as to why jettying was used at all. Perhaps it was to gain more floor area in the cramped conditions of towns (although it is found equally in the countryside). With no gutters or down-pipes to remove surface water, perhaps it was to protect the lower storey from damp, especially the plasterwork, which was typical of a house's construction then. It is also possible that the answer was a structural one. In normal houses, heavy wooden furniture in the centre of a room might cause the joists to sag. The additional joist length, weighted by the wall above pressing down, could perhaps have prevented this? Another possibility was that in dividing the house vertically in this way, timbers could be shorter. The wall-timbers could be just one storey high, not the full height of the house. Perhaps money was at the root of the question after all - with taxes on 'ground area', owners gained 'free space' above! Or perhaps it was simply 'fashion'? The true explanation may have been lost over the centuries, but ideas please!

Alec Clifton-Taylor pronounced: 'Old shop fronts are not a rarity in Bury. Indeed, I cannot recall any other English town which has managed to keep so many shop-fronts that are a real pleasure to look at.' So often modern plate-glass windows have replaced the smaller panes of Georgian and Victorian times. These frequently stand out as unsuitable in a period street. So, well done to Bury St Edmunds for preserving this heritage. Greggs' shop is a little later than 1800 and a Grade I listed building. Bow windows are rare today, but that in the current 'Prezzo's' restaurant still exists. Many will remember this shop as 'Ridleys', with its unusual combination of high glass groceries and a paint department. Here the building is considerably older than the 19th century shop-fronts. Thurlow Champness has an interesting shop-front as well as its fine clock.

In Bury St Edmunds, there is a long tradition of brewing. The monks became experts in this craft and the daily allowance was very generous - eight pints when they were well, half as much again if they were not. They even had a weekly order to deliver 96 gallons to the nuns at Theford! At least this order was for the weakest of the three beers, which they also sold to the Bury citizens. The second strongest was for the brethren and the top grade for visiting dignitaries. Other breweries followed here in Bury, culminating in the present firm of Greene King.

The meeting of Mr Greene with Mr King was a significant day in the history of East Anglian brewing. It was June 1st 1887 when the St Edmunds Brewery, under Frederick King, merged with the nearby Westgate Brewery under Edward Greene. Frederick King had been brewing in Bury since 1868. The Greene family's involvement is less precisely dated, but was around 1799. It was after Benjamin Greene (great grandfather of the writer Graham Greene) returned from London, following his training at Whitbread's. When Edward Green died in 1891, the Bury and Norwich Post declared:

'He was one of the first country brewers to discover that beer need not be vile, black, turgid stuff, but brewed a bright amber-coloured liquid of Burton-type, which he sold at a shilling per gallon and made a fortune.' With the reputation of the monks as excellent brewers, and with the Abbey dominating the town for so many centuries, it is appropriate that a major product of this company is Abbot Ale. Not surprisingly, it is claimed that the water for brewing still comes from the same 11th century source. Outside the very informative Visitors' Centre is an example of a 'mash tun', the vessel used for combining the milled grain (for example malted barley) with other grains and water; this mixture is then heated to make the mash.

These pages and previous page: Bury has two rivers, beautifully named the Lark and the Linnet. The Lark passes under the Abbot's Bridge, which dates from the late 12th century, with additional breakwaters of two centuries later. Portcullises could be lowered to prevent entry. The modern 'gate bridge' to the Abbey grounds serves pedestrians.

Charles Dickens stayed at The Angel when he gave his dramatic readings in the town. He enjoyed his visits, just as his creation Samuel Pickwick had:

'Is this Bury St Edmunds?'
'It is,' replied Mr Pickwick. The coach rattled through the well-paved streets of a handsome little town, of thriving and cleanly appearance, and stopped before a large inn, situated in a wide open street, nearly facing the old abbey. 'And this,' said Mr Pickwick, looking up, 'is the Angel! We alight here, Sam.'

[Chapter16, The Pickwick Papers].

Three previous inns have stood on this site and its history as a coaching inn stretches back to 1452. The present building dates from 1774-6 and was designed by M. Redgrave. The Angel has welcomed a cross section of travellers to Bury, from pilgrim days onwards. It is a famous list - plus those of us not in that category, but who are appreciative nevertheless of hospitality spiced by centuries of practice. In addition to many period features, the building retains a splendid 12th/13th century undercroft which is still in use. For many years horse-drawn coaches departed regularly from The Angel, bound for London.

Elections in former times were colourful affairs and usually involved The Angel Hotel, as James Oakes diary for 1796 recalls:

'The town was exceedingly full, but no sort of irregularity or mischief ensued, nor a pane of glass broke. Beer as usual was given away in different parts of the town and the newly elected members, just before dinner, from the windows of The Angel, threw among the populace each ten guineas in sixpence.' Before the Reform Act, only members of the Bury Corporation were allowed the vote.

Bury St Edmunds once had the honour of claiming the Guiness 'smallest pub' title - 'The Nutshell', in The Traverse. It has unfortunately yielded that title to a pub in the USA. Into the Nutshell's 15ft by 7ft bar it has crowded 102 assorted humans and one Jack Russell. The pub is a timber-framed Grade II listed building which at times has been an ironmonger's, a greengrocer's, a newspaper shop and mostly since 1873, an alehouse. For a time the publican combined pawn-broking. Articles, it is said, would be pawned to pay for the next round of drinks. Relics include a mummified cat, a part skeleton and a ceiling full of foreign banknotes. Not surprisingly it has a sensible tradition of 'no dusting' and like all good pubs it has a ghost or two - notably a monk and a nun.

At the junction of Hollow Road with Barton Road stands an ornate window that is said to have originated in the Medieval Leper Hospital of St Petronilla, in Southgate Street. This 15th century window, with its three 'lights', belongs now to a house on the site of another former hospital - that of St Nicholas in Eastgate. At one time there were six such hospitals in Bury, but 'hospital' in the earlier sense of the word, more closely resembling an almshouse, rather than specifically medical. The remains of St Saviour's Hospital is on Fornham Road, opposite the station. St Stephen's was in Eastgate, St Peter's in Out Risbygate and St John's in Southgate Street.

The St Peter's or Risbygate Cross, now in the grounds of West Suffolk College, formerly stood on the pavement in Risbygate Street to where it was moved in 1878. What is left is an octagonal cross-base of Purbeck stone, set on a rougher block. This cross was one of five showing the boundary of what was known as the 'Banleuca'. It was granted to the Abbey in AD 945 and was the land surrounding by one mile the shrine of St Edmund. This stone is sometimes known as the 'Plague Stone'. The details of the story are that when 'plague' was rampant, usually bubonic plague, known as the 'Black Death' - but also in 1677 smallpox - the small socket hole in the stone was filled with vinegar, so that those returning from the town's market could wash their coins and thus stop the infection spreading. Equally, if a part of the town was isolated, the healthy traders would leave their goods by the stone to be collected by the sick, who would in turn leave their payment there. There are other plague stones dotted around the country. That at Friar's Gate near Derby is sometimes called the 'vinegar stone'. Other examples are at Sutton, near Macclesfield, Birchall, near Leek, and Feltwell in Norfolk. Pedestrians walking past the college may be unaware that a piece of Bury's medieval history is now sited in the gardens there.

The remains of St Saviour's gateway. One of the medieval hospitals of Bury.

Duke Humphrey of Gloucester, brother of King Henry V died in Bury St Edmunds (possibly murdered).

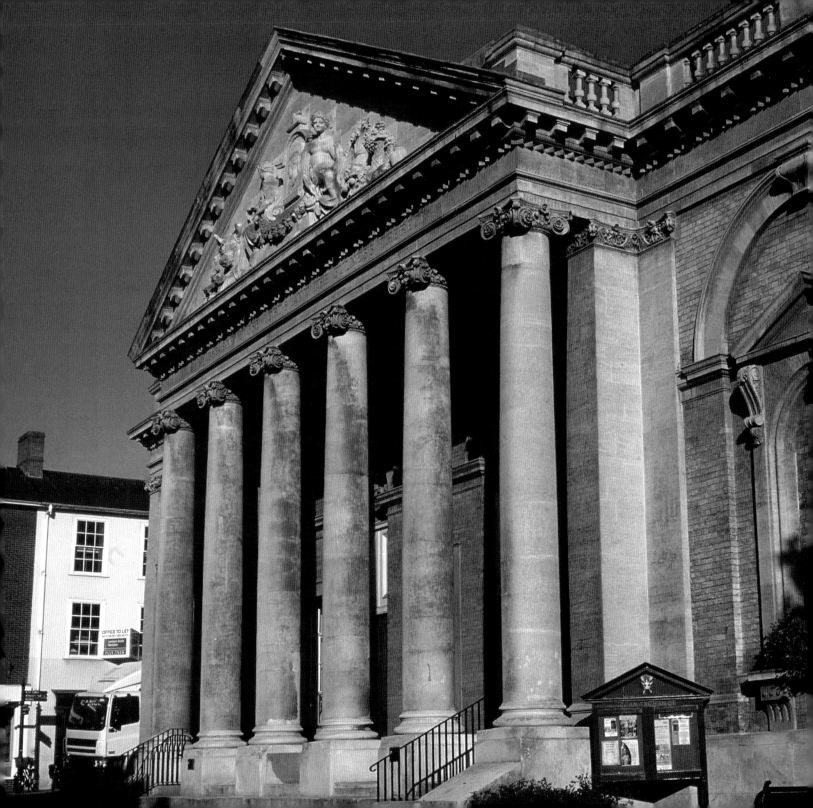

There are three major buildings on Cornhill, and interestingly, all three have been associated with the corn trade.

The first Corn Exchange was built in 1583 (site unknown) by the Guildhall Feoffment Trust and destroyed in Bury's disastrous fire of 1608. It was replaced by a timber 'market cross' on the site of the present building. The description of the building as a 'market cross' is a little confusing! This new building consisted of an open corn hall below and a clothiers' hall above. So, the 'Market Cross' was the first Corn Hall, but was outgrowing its home. In 1836 the Town Council built a new Corn Exchange next door. The same thing eventually happened, and this building also became too small for the expanding corn market.

The present Corn Exchange was built in 1861-2, on the site of the town 'Shambles'. It was designed by Ellis and Woodard and built by the local builder Lot Jackaman, at a cost of £7,000. The front of this Corn Exchange has an impressive six-column pediment, with figures representing agriculture. Unbelievably the idea was mooted in 1959 to pull the Corn Exchange down. Its most recent reincarnation is as a smart pub.

The second building, seen today, was then used as a provision market, with the centre section occupied by a school of dancing and the southern end by a fire station. In the days when this building was a fire station, Bury then saw fire engines and uniforms of a different order. It boasted in late Victorian days, three engines, 24 firemen and 1500 ft. of hose. These were the men with brass helmets and fire engines to match. In the past, before municipal fire stations were set up, the ability to call an engine could be determined by which 'insurance' company you subscribed to. The important badge on the wall would make all the difference as to whether your house was saved or not. These 'firemarks' are now rare but one for the 'Royal' company can be seen on the northern side of Abbeygate Street. In 1937 the public library was opened in this building and finally it was converted into shops.

In 1734 the clothiers' hall was converted into a playhouse and in 1779 the 'Market Cross' was completely re-modeled, on a cruciform plan, by Robert Adam, taking on today's appearance. The ground floor was left open and continued to be used as a corn hall. The builder has been suggested as Thomas Singleton who certainly carved the fine decorative plaques representing for example Pan and King Midas, reminding us of the building's former use.

No longer does St Mary's Square ring to the sounds of its medieval market. It is a beautiful backwater, apart from cars. Its claim to fame is shown in the plaque to Thomas Clarkson, promoter of the Slavery Emancipation Bill of 1833. Wilberforce presented the bill in Parliament with Clarkson as a major supporter.

The Bury 'Fort', in reality the former gaol (1805), lies back from the Sudbury Road, and is screened by a remaining stone façade. The builder was the architect George Byfield, who afterwards designed a house for the Czar of Russia. The brick 'fort' is octagonal. The stonework of the facade is designed to create deep shadows (rustication) but in addition, on the central gateway, the stone has been carved in such a way to give the impression of worm tracks (vermiculation)! A fascinating insight into the old gaol and the town as well, is included in a book entitled 'Adventures with Phantoms' by R. Thurston Hopkins (1884-1958). Hopkins' father was an official with the Commissioners of Prisons and when Bury gaol was vacated he purchased the property. The family then lived in the Governor's house. His son remembered the sombre, echoing old house, and the black frame with the faded letter written by the murderer William Corder. He also remembered the library with its secret cupboard. 'The entrance was through a dummy Corinthian pillar which opened on concealed springs. This hide-out was a family secret and my father, with the rest of the family, made a childish game of mystifying guests or callers by going into the room a little before them and then disappearing.' His father had the skull of William Corder wrapped in a silk handkerchief and coming out of the 'Angel' one day tripped, and the skull rolled out at the feet of Lady Gage!

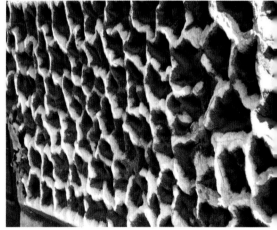

There is really nothing morbid about a stroll through an ancient graveyard. Whatever the season they are atmospheric places, full of interest. Wild flowers adorn the stones and the inscriptions are worth a minute or two of study. Our forebears were keener than us on 'memento mori', the reminder of our mortality. The workmanship on ancient gravestones is often superb and Bury has many fine examples in what is called 'The Great Churchyard/ Great Cemetery', between St Mary's and the Cathedral. So, sit under these mature trees and enjoy the sunlight on mellow stone. Read a name or two in passing and glean part of a life story perhaps?

Above: Henry Crabb Robinson (1775-1867) was an English lawyer and journalist, born in Bury St Edmunds. He was part of a wide circle of 'men of letters' in this country and Germany, and he knew Goethe and Schiller, Wordsworth and Coleridge. He was also one of the founders of London University. Crabb Robinson was known as a diarist and his diaries were published. They give a fascinating perspective on the period. He had associations with this delightful house on the southern border of the town, which is called Linnet House.

Right: Unlike Kent, East Anglia is not the home of oast houses, but this once belonged to the brewery, and has been very successfully converted for domestic use.

Few schools can boast a name more intertwined with history than that of the 'Guildhall Feoffment Community Primary School' in Bridewell Lane. The ancient word 'feoffment' (15th century) means a grant of land and the Guildhall was where the Trustees met. One Jankyn Smyth bequeathed land and properties in trust in 1473, for certain defined purposes. One was to keep his 'anniversary' in St Mary's. A few years later, in 1477, a similar grant to the same Trust was made by one Margaret Odeham. Her bequests included 'saying mass to the prisoners in Bury gaol, and for finding seven faggots of wood weekly, from Hallowe'en to Easter, for the prisoners in the long ward of the gaol.' Her philanthropy was doubtless much appreciated. Because the Trust was in being, the mechanics of adding similar gifts were in place. In the 200 years following the original gifts, many more followed. By Queen Victoria's accession the Trust was worth over £2,000. But its responsibilities were now enormous: repairing the Guildhall, the Shire Hall and the Borough Bridewell; 22 public and private pumps to look after, plus five wells and many almshouses that had been specified. In addition, all the houses, farms and other buildings let to tenants, numbering by 1838 over 60.

Education has been important in the history of the Trust. In 1939-40 a decision was taken to build no less than three schools: The Guildhall Commercial School, The Guildhall Feoffment School for Poor Boys and The Guildhall Feoffment School for Poor Girls. The architect for the first two was Mr Henry Kendall of London. His requirements were exacting, for example the number of knots allowed per yard of timber! John Trevethan, a local builder, was granted the contract to build the schools. The Head of the Boys' school was a Mr Fuller. His salary in 1843 when the school opened, was £70 per annum and the 27 pupils payed one penny per week. Together with the usual academic studies, garden husbandry was on the curriculum for the boys, and land was rented for this. In the Girls' school, knitting, sewing and laundry replaced the husbandry. A laundry was built at the school to assist this training. The Commercial School pupils had a tougher regime, and a higher academic record was expected. The progress of the school was rapid and by 1891, in the Boys' school alone, there were 400

pupils and additional buildings were needed. By 1907 the Head, Mr John Timpson, had six assistants, and the number on roll peaked at 503.

In the 1920s the schools were taken over by the Local Education Authority and in 1936 the Guildhall Feoffment Junior Mixed School was created. In the 1970s the Guildhall Feoffment County Primary School (ages 5-9) was set up, the forerunner of today's school.

The red brick and stone twin towers (previously linked by an overall roof) of Bury's former G.E.R. station would not look out of place in Venice! Railway companies often tried to create an image of respectability and confidence. Norwich Thorpe was built in the 'French chateau' style, and the Musee D'Orsay in Paris, in the grand palace style. The 'Venetian look' is perhaps not too far-fetched, as the architect, Sancton Wood (1816-86), was also commissioned by the Great Southern and Western Railway Company, in Ireland, to design Dublin's re-named Heuston Station (formerly Kingsbridge Street). This 1846 station (Bury's was opened in 1847) was certainly the most impressive in Dublin and was said to have been based upon an Italian Palazzo, with Corinthian columns and domed campaniles. Three hundred people were entertained at 'The Angel' to celebrate the station's opening.

There was a second G.E.R. Station called Eastgate Street (Bury St Edmunds, Eastgate) operating from 1865-1909 and briefly in 1914.

Because many railwaymen worked such 'unsocial hours', and might be prevented from attending normal church services, the Railway Mission was set up in 1881. At first they would meet anywhere they could, including waiting rooms and even engine sheds, as an inter-denominational church. It was in 1895 that a group of Bury railwaymen approached Mrs Arthur Ridley (a Congregationalist) to ask if she would form a branch of the Railway Mission as Superintendant and the good lady rose to the challenge. Their first meetings were in the stationmaster's house but when they needed more space, a corrugated iron hall was built, at a cost of £317. 7s. 7d. Bury's 'tin tabernacle' became the Mission's church, and was opened by the Mayor in May 1900. Today there is still an International Railway Mission but Bury's Grade 11 listed building has been, from 2002, the home of the Seventh-day Adventist Church.

A reminder that 'looking up' often reveals some interesting additions to the townscape.

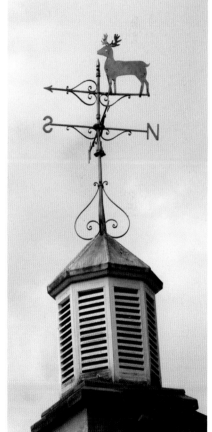

Not everyone has liked the architecture of St John's and the forthright Nikolaus Pevsner was not kind, particularly regarding its spire. Unfortunately bad opinions can be infectious. However it has also been described as 'one of the first great Victorian Gothic churches in England' (Simon Knott). Seen from a distance, against a fitting sky, it is certainly impressive, with the massive spire and flying buttresses. It was built to a design of William Ranger, using the local 'Woolpit Whites'. St John's was consecrated in 1841 and has remained part of the Anglo Catholic tradition within the Anglican Church. St John's was substantially changed during the incumbency of Father Stewart Holland during the 1870s. The old box pews were removed, as was the great pulpit; the west gallery was demolished and the chancel was tiled. A great reredos was fitted and earlier coloured glass replaced by plain. When St John's was built, much of the area called 'Brackland' was yet to be developed. Today the church can still be viewed from a distance, but now very much as part of its Victorian and early 20th century environment.

'Brackland' the Victorian development, is a 'homely area with small 'villagey' shops.' (A. C-T.). Its character is somewhat different to the rest of Bury, as in St John's Street for example. Long may this variety of attractive premises remain.

The Quakers or 'Society of Friends' was started by George Fox in the mid 17th century and formally organized in 1667. In Bury St Edmunds his followers have had a continuous presence for 350 years, and their meeting house in St John's Street (1750) is one of the oldest in Suffolk. Like most 'non-conformist' assemblies, the Quakers were not officially allowed to be buried in Anglican churchyards, although in the early days a few were. The alternatives were to use their own land, or set up their own burial grounds by purchase. They were efficient at keeping registers of births, deaths and marriages, which have been collated for research purposes. They also complied with the 'Burial in Woollen' Acts 1666-80. The burial of non-conformists, such as Quakers, by their own ministers, was finally permitted as late as 1880, after which some non-conformist burial grounds were closed. Their gravestones are identical in form.

Bury's Unitarian Chapel in Churchgate Street (1711-12) is a magnificent Grade1 listed building, of glowing orangey-red brickwork. It is in Stretcher Bond (partly), where every course consists of stretchers only. Inside, it boasts a 'two tier' pulpit. It is still owned by the Unitarian Trustees, with services on the first Sunday afternoon of each month. But in addition, it is available for a wide range of events, from music, to receptions, talks and also weddings.

No. 2, Crown Street, close to the Norman Tower, and facing Chequer Square, is a wonderful mix of mock-Tudor. This turreted house was built in 1846 at a cost of £2,300, a large sum of money in early Victorian times. It has large Tudor-style chimneys and oriel (protruding) windows on both sides, with the brick pattern called 'diapering'. This is usually where bricks of a different colour are placed to form a repeated pattern of squares or diamonds. The date is included in the design of the house. The architect was Mr Cottingham and the builder was Thomas Farrow, both of whom were involved in the restoration of the Norman Tower. It was the office for a Savings Bank (sometimes called 'The Penny Bank') which had at its height 3,000 investors.

Chequer Square (previously 'Paddock Pond'), with its building variety, is an elegant corner of the town, close to the Cathedral and the Norman Tower. On the southern side it includes some delightful ornamental balconies. On its northern side is a building whose previous life was as the 'Six Bells' Inn. Its brick exterior, as so often, hides a timber building, probably dating from the 17th century. Look for a house of importance in this square called the Baret Huse, reputedly owned by a medieval clothier, John Baret.

Where does reality end and the shadows start?

Cupola House, in The Traverse, deceptively timber-framed, has been described as 'the best 17th century house of Bury' (N.P.). It was built in 1693 for a wealthy apothecary called Thomas Macro. It is three storeys high and graced by a cupola. This feature (sometimes known as a 'belvedere') was fashionable at the time. It was often built in the garden as a 'pleasure house' or, as in Bury, a lookout on the top of a house.

Celia Fiennes (1662-1741), was the daughter of a colonel in Cromwell's army. She is famous for the journeys she made and her descriptions of them. Between 1684-1703, accompanied by two servants, she rode sidesaddle through every county of England. With the roads and dangers of her time it was a remarkable feat, and her comments shed light at first hand upon a fascinating chapter of our history. Much of her writing was left until the journeying was over. It was fortunate that Bury St Edmunds was included in her itinerary and that Celia Fiennes visited Cupola House. The first complete edition of her book appeared in 1888 under the title 'Through England on a Side Saddle'. Celia Fiennes wrote:

'The high house is an apothecary's - at least 60 steps up from the ground - and gives a pleasing prospect of the whole town. This house is the new mode of building: four rooms of a floor pretty sizeable and high, well furnished, a drawing room and chamber full of china and a damask bed, embroidered. Two other rooms, Camlet and mohair beds; a pretty deal of plate in his wife's chambers and parlours below, and a large shop.'

In June 2012, Cupola House suffered a terrible fire, but should rise from the ashes.

Gracious houses constructed in fashionable white brick, with their front gardens in evidence. Well Street is so full of interesting houses.

Before the end of the 18th century the tried and tested red bricks that had served our towns so well for generations, started to go 'out of fashion'. Whatever is scarce (and probably dear) is sought after, to impress one's neighbours. So-called 'white' bricks, which were often a shade of yellow, started to be used in quantity. Perhaps the greater similarity to stone was an attraction. Sometimes the sides of the houses were built still in red bricks, with the more fashionable whites at the front, and sometimes the two colours were juxtaposed (see Clarkson's house in St Mary's Square). Bury was luckier than some towns in having a ready source of this different clay locally available, especially in Woolpit and Culford. The 'white' bricks are often referred to as 'Woolpit Whites' but Culford bricks were closer to white in colour. 'Woolpit Whites are reputed to have travelled to Washington to be used in the Capitol building, but the story is not confirmed. The clay for 'whites' has more lime in its composition, and little iron, so bricks remain much paler.

Opposite: A recent addition to Bury's street scene is the large shopping centre built adjoining St Andrew's Street, under the auspices of 'arc' developments. The site was that of the former Cattle Market and has given some modern architectural opportunities, including a striking design for Debenham's store. The previous modern addition, a few years earlier, was Cornhill Walk

Below: Like it or hate it, the sugar factory has been part of Bury St Edmunds' skyline since 1925. Run by the British Sugar Corporation, it can process 14,000 tonnes of sugar beet per day from 1000 UK growers. This view is from the railway station.

An elegant Risbygate Terrace and brick variations in The Traverse. This five-house terrace has an unusual parapet along the roof line, and additional ornamentation. The date is mid-nineteenth century.

This building, (previously the street was called Long Brackland), was at one time a public house called the 'Lamb and Flag'. It has an attractive carved beam along its street face.

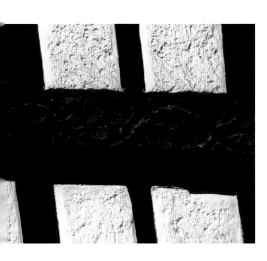

On 16th August 1646 Bury St Edmunds' Congregational Chapel (now United Reform) was founded, by five men, three women and six children. It claims to be the oldest continuously worshipping Non-conformist chapel in the town. Its congregation met at other venues until land was acquired in Whiting Street as early as 1697. This building, known then as 'The Independent Chapel' was finished by 1708. Increasing numbers led to extensions to the chapel, and a school-room was added in 1851. The Victorian 'gothic' front was completed in 1866. A memorial outside commemorates Elias Thacker and John Copping, who died for their faith. They were hanged in the reign of Elizabeth I for spreading 'independent' views in pamphlets.

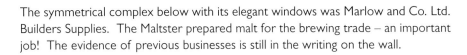

The symmetrical complex below with its elegant windows was Marlow and Co. Ltd. Builders Supplies. The Maltster prepared malt for the brewing trade – an important job! The evidence of previous businesses is still in the writing on the wall.

Adjoining the Post Office on Cornhill is an amazingly-decorated building of the early 20th century with a large amount of timbering and the incorporation of statues of kings, including King Canute at the top, getting his feet wet. It was commissioned by Sir Jesse Boot of Boot's Chemists from Michael Vine Treleavan. One expert has described it this way: 'the building bursts forth into a glorious riot of mock timber-framing and stucco ornamentation' (A.C-T.).

The 'finishing off' of a gable end or gable window by the use of barge-boards is a functional application that has also been used as an attractive feature. Practically, the roof timbers in that area are hidden and protected by the barge-board, but its ornate design often adds a great deal to the roof of a building. Bury has many attractive examples.

The Suffolk Regimental Museum is housed at 'The Keep' at Gibraltar Barracks in Bury.

In 1954 Colonel Robert Ogilby founded the Army Museums Ogilby Trust. Colonel Ogilby believed that 'the fighting spirit of the British soldier stemmed from the 'esprit de corps' engendered by the Army's regimental structure'. This belief underpinned his work. Public support for these museums can make a considerable impact on the preservation of the nation's military heritage. The museum in Bury includes displays of uniforms, weapons, regimental trophies, badges, insignia and musical items. Regiments represented are: The Royal Anglian Regiment; The Suffolk Regiment; The 12th (or East Suffolk) Regiment of Foot; The Duke of Norfolk's Regiment of Foot; The Cambridgeshire Regiment TA.

Lot Jackaman was a local builder who in 1861-2 took on the enormous task of constructing the new Corn Exchange. His own very unusual 'show-house' is opposite the brewery. Lot was also responsible for building the town's first swimming pool. He died in 1885, aged 70.

Opposite: In the Middle Ages, and for sometime afterwards, the general inability to read made a townscape rather different from today. Traders relied upon visual signs and three-dimensional objects to sell their wares. The traditional chemists' shops may still occasionally display the bottles of coloured water or, as here, a large mortar and pestle to represent their profession. This example in Abbeygate Street reminds us that apothecaries, and later chemists, were based here. Marie Cressener is listed as an apothecary in 17th century Bury and it is also on record that a mortar and pestle originally occupied the St Edmund 'niche' at the top of Abbeygate Street. In Georgian times onwards, with many horses passing by, boot-scrapers were a reminder of the state of the roads. Clean streets are a comparatively modern feature of our towns but some of the old boot-scrapers have survived in Bury.

Right: It is good that items such as period petrol pumps should be preserved. This one is probably from the 1940s and is part of Hawkes' showroom in Mustow Street. How many of us can remember these 'cranked' petrol pumps with the handles going backwards and forwards? They are certainly museum objects now.

Medieval Guilds were in one sense like modern Trade Unions. In Bury St Edmunds there were as many as 17 different guilds historically. They controlled the work ethic of local trades and crafts and made sure young apprentices were properly trained. Many guilds had a religious rather than a purely craft element. They might play a part in local celebrations, perhaps vying with other guilds for the most elaborate costumes. In Bury St Edmunds, the Guildhall, in Guildhall Street, dates from pre 15th century (a stone doorway inside the porch is 200 years older). After the demise of the medieval guilds it was the meeting place of the Corporation from 1606, the Improvement Commissioners from 1811 and the Borough Council until as late as 1966. The porch has a fine stone coat of arms, together with chequer-work patterning at the top, made up of limestone and knapped flint, set in squares. Between this and the doorway is a banded section of flint and red brick. The sides of the porch (characteristically, and also for example with flint buildings) used less-refined materials than on the public face of the building.

Tucked into the north-west corner of Angel Hill ('Angel Corner') is an attractive early 18th century house that was once the beautiful setting for Bury's clock museum, as well as its former Record Office. 'The Clock House' has one hopper-head dated 1702 and another with the initals HG, after Henry Goodman, who built the property.

The former Borough Council Offices on Angel Hill, now housing the Bury St Edmunds' Town Council Offices, were built in 1935-7 to a design by the English architect Basil Oliver (1882-1948). It was in the 'Neo-Georgian' style and described by Pevsner as 'tactful and completely uneventful'! In this building Oliver acted more as 'consultant' architect to W. H. Mitchell of 'Mitchell and Weston'. Oliver was a late 'Arts and Crafts' exponent, beyond the movement's time. He was commissioned to design inns for Greene King, whose houses then added appropriate fittings by the 'Art Workers Guild', in the 'Arts and Crafts' style. The building was sold in 2009.

A splendid example of another skill, that of brick carving, can be seen in the Café Rouge in Abbeygate Street. Here the mortar joints are naturally very thin.

Further examples can be seen where bricks of different shades or colours have been combined. Brick-making before the introduction of machine-made bricks, was never a precise craft. Some parts of the kiln fired hotter than others and bricks were sometimes 'over-cooked'. Very effective use has been made of these colour variations and they came to be created deliberately.

Not far from Bury St Edmunds is a very unusual hand-made brick-yard, at Bulmer Tye, near Sudbury ('The Bulmer Brick and Tile Co.'). Specialist orders come from all over the world, and from almost every major building that includes bricks in its structure. It is an education in itself to visit this yard, with its ancient round open-air kilns and its 'library' of wooden brick moulds. [Visitors are welcome by appointment.]

Pargeting is a speciality of Suffolk and Essex in particular and there are examples in Bury St Edmunds of this work. Essentially it is the creation of incised patterns in clay over the surface of a wall, or similar designs in relief.

Although tile-hanging is not especially associated with East Anglia, examples do occur in Bury St Edmunds. It probably started in the late 17th century and had the practical purpose of protecting the walls against bad weather - hence another name 'weather-tiling'. The plain tiles used are the same as roofing tiles but the more ornate tiles create attractive patterns. If the wall is of brick, wooden battens or pegs are used, but many buildings covered in this way are timber-framed, and the tiles are supported on oak laths. Often the upper floor only is covered, or perhaps just a gable-end. Tile-hung walls can be seen at the 'Rose and Crown' in Westgate Street, in the Traverse at the premises of Gerald Boughton, and also in the Thomas Cook building in Abbeygate Street.

The Maynewater area (sometimes Maidwater or Maidenwater) remained in earlier times an independent unit within the town of Bury, part of what was called the 'Honour of Clare'. A very large estate across East Anglia had been granted by a grateful William the Conqueror to Richard Fitz-Gilbert, one of the Norman barons.

Along Maynewater Lane is the attractive Square, built in 1868 by the philanthropist Edward Greene, as a group of 16 houses, to accommodate workers from the brewery. They were tied cottages, and surprisingly for the time, they had all mod cons - three bedrooms, two communal pumps and an outside privy each!

The Abbeygate Street clock, above the premises of Thurlow Champness, was made in Leeds and has been a feature of the street for many decades. Thurlow Champness has an attractive shop front.

Details of the Crown Street entrance door to the Cathedral and ornamental woodwork as part of the jettying of a house in Eastgate, believed to have been moved from Mustow Street.

This page and opposite: Flints are found across East Anglia (and other areas such as Sussex). Often flints are used as 'from the fields', uncut, but sometimes they are 'coursed' or 'sized'. At other times, and Bury has examples, the flints are cut open, or knapped, to show the shiny interiors, black, among a number of colours. Flints are often used in conjunction with brick or stone and this gets over the problem of the irregular flint-stones being used to create corners. Aesthetically, these combinations of materials and colours can work very well. (See also page 89 for flint work).

Opposite: Pantiles are a feature of East Anglian towns and villages. The tiles are large ones, having a single lap downwards and a 'hook' over the next tile across. No other fixing is used and they stay in place by their own weight through almost every weather condition. They create an attractive 'wave' pattern of shadows with the sun on them. Slates are also seen in Bury, more typically as the roof material in Victorian or 20th century buildings. The advent of the railways made it possible, for example, for slates to be brought from Wales.

A small selection of the stonework that can be observed around the town. How many can you find?

Flowers in any context lift the spirits and
framed by railings have added interest.

Opposite: Ash Cottage is approximately 600 years old and was originally a 'one up, one down' building, with a fire in the middle of the floor. Its vast fireplace was put in after the Reformation. It was built it is said, with stones from the former abbey. The main room has outstanding carved beams, evidence of the wealth of a former owner.

The Bury Post Office is a fine building, with its origins in the Victorian period. This very new-looking office was opened in 1896. Look up at the interesting pediment that crowns the outside, showing Queen Victoria's coat of arms.

Pubs stretch back a long way: Romans had their taverns (tavernae) and Saxons their alehouses. Today, an assortment of names is used, and the distinctions are not always obvious. In early times, when few could read, inn signs were very important. The Romans hung vine leaves outside their taverns as a sign that drinks were available. In England the equivalent was a long pole or 'ale-stake' covered in evergreens, as the sign that beer was served. Two centuries ago Bury was reputed to support 150 pubs.

It was important that pub signs were displayed and today they are a colourful reminder of our history. Bury's fine 'Elephant and Castle' sign in Hospital Road (don't cross the busy road alone) is taken from the crest of the Cutlers' Company, one of the Livery Companies of the City of London. It gave this name to the Newington area and to a station. Ivory featured in the trade of the

company, and it is also reminiscent of earlier days when elephants would carry a small castle on going into battle.

'The Rose and Crown' (Westgate Street) is of course a royal device in the same way that in former times the Bury 'Cross Keys' (of St Peter) was a religious one. The attractive sign for the 'Dog and Partridge' (previously 'The Mermaid') in Crown Street, graces a timber-framed building of the 17th century or earlier, famed for its Rook Pie. In previous generations the pub had a regular visit from the local handbell-ringing team. A fierce concoction called Ringers'Mix (a secret combination of various ales) was left in a four gallon pitcher for ringers to help themselves! Legend does not report on the likely dire effects upon their ringing! The previously named 'Rising Sun' in Risbygate Street (now St Edmund's Tavern), whose history stretches back to the 15th century, had the debateable honour of housing Cromwell for a night. St John's Street still has 'The Bushel', meaning a pre-decimalization unit of measure, well known to a farming community. It represented '8 gallons' in the dry measuring of corn or fruit. This pub was a former coaching inn, at one time named 'The White Rose'. 'The Masons' Arms' in Whiting Street, with its 'Essex' weather-boarding, refers to another Livery Company, the Masons of the City of London, and part of their heraldic device is a pair of compasses as seen on their pub sign. In 1780, one previous landlady of 'The Masons' Arms' advertised in the Ipswich Journal that she was now running the pub on her own (Mr John Bumstead and his son being deceased):

Sarah Bumstead 'intends to sell spirituous liquors . . . and having laid in a fresh stock of the best brandies, rum, Holland and common gin, she respectfully solicits the favours of all former customers.' And its hospitality continues today, still with 'spirituous liquors'.

The 'Fox' in Eastgate was a drovers' inn, one of the oldest in Bury. Drovers would stop off here and take a drink while their animals took advantage of the ford opposite. They had stabling for 100 horses in those early days and for entertainment there was reputed to be a ducking stool on the riverbank opposite!'

Another notable pub in Guildhall Street is the 'Black Boy', a reminder of a cruel period for children.

Pub signs change – and noy always for the better. It is sometimes good to remember old favourites.

[For those interested in the subject of pub and inn signs, there is an Inn Sign Society.]

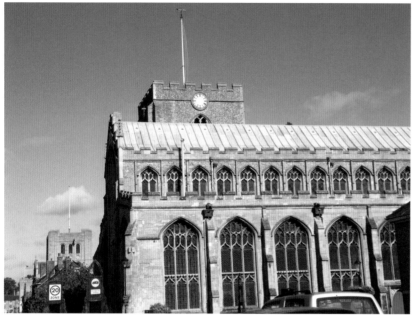

The present St Mary's Church, the third largest parish church in the country, with a 213 ft. nave, was completed in 1427. It was one of three such churches within the precincts of the Abbey. St James's and St Margaret's (demolished) were the other two. St Mary's holds the grave of Mary Tudor, sister of Henry VIII, who was first married to King Louis XII of France and subsequently, after his death, secretly married to Charles Brandon, Duke of Suffolk. The Mary Tudor Window was presented by Queen Victoria. St Mary's west window is also the largest in the country. St Mary's roof is justifiably famous, with its alternating hammer beams, and angel figures. There are also carvings of dragons, unicorns, birds and fish for example. It is regarded as the 'civic church' of Bury, but there is little evidence of the original Norman building. The church now incorporates the Chapel of the Suffolk Regiment.

In 'Bloody' Mary's reign, 17 Protestant martyrs were hanged in Bury St Edmunds. A monument was erected in 1903 near the then St James's church in their memory. A similar memorial to religious martyrs can be found outside the Congregational Church (now United Reform).

Chimneys are not given due credit as the dramatic and revolutionary feature in the history of houses that they truly are! Before their advent a 'smoke-hole' in the roof was the usual method of allowing smoke to disperse. But for all sorts of reasons it was never efficient, and rooms were often smoke-filled. Chimneys, at a stroke, allowed upper storeys to be built because they channeled the smoke away to the roof. They also gave the world the opportunity for attractive and unusual embellishments on the roof-scape. So, look skywards and give a Mary Poppins nod of approval to the range of chimneys here in Bury.

This two-storey house, now a major museum, is the oldest domestic building in Bury. It is of Norman origin and dates from c1180. It is said to have been built by a member of Bury's Jewish community. In its long history, Moyse's Hall has been many things, including an inn, a bridewell, a gaol, a police station and even a G.E.R parcels office. Since 1899 it has been a museum, and what better use for this ancient building. Its exhibitions include the story of William Corder, murderer of Maria Marten, (The Red Barn); witchcraft; the Suffolk Regiment; coinage; medieval life, murder and superstition. In addition, characters from the past visit the museum, so you may encounter a medieval monk or a medieval craftswoman, or even find that your guide around the building is a Victorian gentleman.

Old towns such as Bury often have long established rights to hold a market. For Bury the charter was given in 1235. The original market area was almost certainly around St Mary's Square, 'The Old Market', before its present site. In the Middle Ages there was a 'Great Market' here, incorporating different specialities and trading groups, such as the cheese market, the butter market and the fish market. Each would have their rows as part of the bigger market, for example the goldsmiths' row, and the glovers' row. The 'Cook's row'(a surname) was where Abbeygate Street stands. Naturally the prudent abbots exacted market tolls from the traders. They even 'sub-contracted' the dung from the streets!

It is a truism to say that flowers will enhance any occasion or any location. When the location is an old English town and the floral displays are set against the backdrop of ancient buildings, there is a sense of harmony from the outset. The 'Britain in Bloom' Campaign, starting in 1963, has run from 2002 under the auspices of the Royal Horticultural Society. It offers the chance of recognition to any community, however large or small, where the addition of flowers, or some impact upon the natural environment, is attempted. In Bury, as elsewhere, the campaign is 'community-led' - a local band of residents, under the 'Bury in Bloom' committee. Here they have made Bury St Edmunds one of Britain's floral towns over some 25 years.

Bury is fortunate in having so elegant a meeting place as The Athenaeum. Since its original creation as the Assembly Rooms it has served a multitude of functions, from the reception of Royalty (as following the Maundy Service of 2009), to the packed buying frenzy of the crowded Christmas market. Its two-storeyed façade of 1804 was by Francis Sandys (1788-1814) and its ballroom attributed to Robert Adam. It is a grand building by any standards and not surprisingly, Grade I listed. Sandys was an Irish-born architect whose career flourished in the service of Frederick Augustus Hervey, 4th Earl of Bristol and Bishop of Derry. Sandys built the Earl Bishop's house at Ickworth in 1796. Following this he developed his architectural practice around Bury, having previously designed, for example, Finborough Hall, the year before Ickworth. The Athenaeum's dome is a Victorian observatory, no longer used, and probably inadequate to its job. The Athenaeum was originally a pivate home known as 'The White Home'.

The Theatre Royal in Bury has been described as a 'hidden jewel' in the National Trust's crown. It was designed by William Wilkins and built in 1819. It is a Grade I listed building. Wilkins also designed the National Gallery and Downing College, Cambridge. It is held on a 999-year lease by the Trust from the owners, Greene King Brewery. At one time it was a barrel store. It is the last remaining Regency playhouse in Britain and has an important place in the history of the theatre in this country. In addition to its policy of 'restoring the repertoire' of the Georgian theatre, the Theatre Royal offers a wide range of experiences throughout the year. An unusual claim to fame was the theatre's first performance of the ever-popular 'Charley's Aunt' 1892.

In 2009, Bury St Edmunds and its Cathedral were honored by being chosen for the historic Royal Maundy service, on the day before Good Friday. It was a colourful occasion, made especially so by the presence of the 'Beefeaters' in their Tudor uniforms. That year the number of male and female recipients each totalled the Queen's age of 83. They received specially minted maundy money in red and white, long-stringed leather purses.

Bury, somewhat unusually, has a War Memorial dedicated to the town's losses in the Boer War(s). It is a dramatic sculpture, situated in the Market Place, Cornhill. The memorial was designed by A. G. Walker and unveiled by General Lord Methmers on November 11 1904.

Bury St Edmunds Walks

THIS BOOK HAS brought together a wealth of architectural detail as well as historical events in Bury St Edmunds. The five walks that now follow in the town centre show many of the photograph locations and will doubtless reveal many other locations which might have been included - for Bury St Edmunds is an architectural gem.

These short walks need not be tackled all at once, although they are arranged so that the end of one walk is close to the start of the next walk and it is possible all five could be undertaken in one session.

A car route has been added, too, so that locations a little further out can be visited.

Bury's street pattern has remained unaltered in the town centre for centuries, and this allows us to make use of one of the early Ordnance Survey maps of the town centre. It is at a scale of 25 inches to 1 mile, and it will be possible to establish that not only are the streets much the same, but, the building plots, too.

The map used is one of the 'County Series' of maps the Ordnance Survey started working on in the mid 19th century - although many were published in the 1880s and 1890s, with this sheet (XLIV.7) published in 1886. These maps are, arguably, some of the finest maps produced by the Ordnance Survey. Their scale means that virtually every bit of ground detail can be plotted accurately - including buildings and property and field boundaries, roads, paths, etc.

An option on the 1st edition 25 inch maps was hand-colouring. A coloured map was 3/6d or 4/-, whereas a standard map was 2/6d. We are fortunate that the town centre maps of Bury in the Record Office were hand-coloured and they certainly merit closer inspection than the standard black and white printed versions. These maps are works of art, and were mostly hand-coloured by boys who were paid on a piece work basis; later this work was taken on by women.

Because of the almost random distribution of hand-coloured maps that survive, it does not mean that adjoining maps will also be hand-coloured. Nor is it something confined to towns and cities. Many hand-coloured maps were produced of rural areas, with farms and other buildings being coloured, as were roads and waterways.

The colours on sheet XLIV.7 of Bury town centre may not be as vivid as on some maps, and this may be down to storage or use over the years. It is, however, an extremely fine map.

The 25 inch maps continued in production into the 20th century, going through different editions and, today, are still central to the work of the Ordnance Survey, although the scale is now 1:2,500.

Ashley Sampson

Locally called the 'Pillar of Salt',
(a biblical reference) this signpost
stands on Angel Hill in front of Abbey Gate.
It is loved or hated, but does represent an
interesting slice of history as the first
example of a lighted sign post.

It was designed by Basil Oliver in 1935 and is
made of whitewashed concrete and metal.

Walk 1

Metres 0   100   200

Yards 0   100   200

1. Pillar of Salt (p.132)
2. Bow Window (p.42)
3. 'Royal' Insurance badge (p.56)
   *(in passing, note large house on
   corner of Hatter St and Abbeygate
   which had a serious fire and was
   almost destroyed)*
4. Thurlow Champness shop front
   (p.100)
5. Clock (p.100)
6. Mortar and Pestle (p.90)
7. Greggs (p.43)
8. Tile hanging (p.98)
9. St Edmund (p.1) *(in passing,
   note barge-boards on right)*
10. Pargeting (p.97)
11. Brick carving (p.96)
12. Corn Exchange (pp.54-55)
13. 'arc' development (p.80)
14. Old fire station (p.56)
15. Old Town Hall (Market Cross) (p.57)
16. Statues on WHS building (p.86)
17. Victorian Post Office (p.109)
18. Contrasting brick colours (p.82)
19. Cupola House (p.78)
20. Tile Hanging (p.98)
21. 'The Nutshell' pub (pp.50-51)

The Acacias

B.M.162·E

RENT GOVEL STREET

Hotel

Chantry (Site of)

P.H.

P.H.

Police Station

B.M.153·9   B.M.148·1   LOOMS LANE

M.173·3

42

CORNHILL   60 ft. N

17

16   L.B.

Town Hall

15   18

13

173

Hotel

B.M.169·1

Meth. Ch. Wesn.

Burial Ground

HIGH BAXTER STREET

LOWER BAXTER STREET

B.M.122·4

145

B.M.173·0

14   Provision Market

B.M.165·2

BUTTER MARKET

P.H.

ANGEL HILL

B.M.147·6

Start of Walk 1

SKINTER STREET

MEAT MARKET

STALL STREET

B.M.173·0

19

Bank

Start of Walk 2

1.

WOOLHALL STREET

Corn Exchange

B.M.160·1

20

21   D.F.

Hotel

B.M.148·9

3

P.H.

2

Ward

143

Abbeygate

B.M.126·4

Hotel

Und.

167

Ward Boundary

R.W.

12

9   8

10   A B B E Y G A T E   C.R.

7   6   5   4

151

Post Office

Abbey House

126

P.H.

W.M.

Bank

11

B.M.155·7

Banks

Chantry (Site of)

M.166·2

156

153

GUILDHALL STREET

Chantry (Site of)

P.H.

Chantry (Site of)

WHITING STREET

BUTTER STREET

C.R.

Chantry (Site of)

ANGEL LANE

127

Athenaeum (Remains of)

127

St.

B.M.152·5

Guildhall

P.H.

Unitn. Ch.

CHEQUER

Exchequer (Site of)

SQUARE

161

150

Chantry (Site of)

CHURCHGATE   133   STREET

P.H.

B.M.148·6

Chantry (Site of)

B.M.132·3   P.H.

W.M.

B.M.161·4

Lloyds Bank started in about 1765. A button maker called John Taylor joined with an iron dealer called Sampson Lloyd to set up a bank in Birmingham. Bees were known for their hard work, hence the bee-hive, but the black horse was an older sign they inherited on the purchase of a local shop.

Walk 2

| Metres | 0 | | 100 | | 200 |
| Yards | 0 | | 100 | | 200 |

1. The 'Beehive' Bank sign (p.134)
2. Boer War Memorial (Cornhill) (p.130)
3. Moyse's Hall Museum (pp.116–117)
4. 'Mothercare' weather vane (p.67)
5. Risbygate Terrace (p.82)
6. St John's Street shop fronts (pp.70-71)
7. Quaker Meeting House and burial ground (p.72)
8. Beamed former pub, 33 St John's Street (p.83)
9. St John's Church (pp.68-69)
   (In passing, note the brick 'diapering' in Orchard Street)
10. Flint house (p.103)
11. Well St., with delightful doors and windows (p.79)
12. Hedgehog posing (p.90)
13. Methodist interior *(permission needed to view)* (pp.34-35)
14. King's Arms pub sign (p.111)
    - do you know what each part means?

(Look for a fine verandah on a house on the left. It was once called 'The Acacias'.)
15. Venetian window. (p.36)
    Note the ornate gate, too. Same house where Nora Lofts lived. Look for her plaque.
16. Former Methodist church

The Abbey grounds and the Botanic Gardens offer many different routes through the grounds. It may, therefore, be best to suggest that routes are found independently, while trying to find these interesting buildings and structures within the grounds of the former abbey and the newer cathedral.

The following are features to look for in the grounds and in the cathedral in an approximate order. It is suggested that the Gardens are exited through the Abbey Gate and that the cathedral is approached off Angel Hill via an entrance next to Abbey House (see map). See how many you can find.

The house is named after Alwyne, who was the monk who accompanied Edmund's body to London for safety from the Danes.

Walk 3

| Metres | 0 | | | | | | | | 100 | | | | 200 |
| Yards | 0 | | | | | | | 100 | | | | 200 | |

1. Alwyn's House (p.136)
2. Abbot's Bridge (p.46)
   In passing look at Model of Abbey and grounds
3. Abbey ruins (p.31)
   (Can you find the Chapter House and what it was used for, and also where King John's barons met) In passing, note the Memorial Gardens
4. Abbey Gate (p.27)
   Turn left off street immediately past Abbey House (white building)
5. Mosaic (p.10)
6. Godspeed V (p.11)

Enter cathedral by back door from cloisters

7. Among many things to see, look out for
   a) stained glass window showing Garden of Eden (pp.18–19)
   b) chandelier (p.20)
   c) new tower ceiling (p.21)
   d) recycled heating grills (p.20)
   e) boot scraper outside on pavement (p.90)
8. Norman Tower (pp.24-25)
9. Chimneys & Oriel windows at no.2, Crown St (pp.74-75)
10. Marian Martyr's monument (p.113)
11. Modern statue of St Edmund (by Frink) (p.26)
12. Houses in arches of former abbey (p.28)
13. Clopton's Asylum (p.30)
14. Charnel House (p.30)
15. Walk the graveyard route to St Mary's Church, and through gate onto the pavement (to right of the view in the photograph on p.112)
16. St Mary's Church, from Crown Street (p.112)
17. Inside St Mary's, look for the plaque to Mary Tudor (p.112) and the fine nave roof

The house named 'St Denys' in Honey Hill is striking in its architecture. The name may have been taken from an earlier chapel associated with the Abbey. Apart from the fort, it is almost the only stone-constructed building in Bury - so very rare in this brick and timber town.

Walk 4

1. St Denys (p.138)
2. St Mary's Square (p.58)
3. Clarkson's House (p.58)
4. Bath Cottage (p.102)
5. Traction engine weather vane (p.67)
6. Maynewater Square (p.99)
7. Jackaman's plaque and house (p.89)
8. Theatre Royal (permission needed to view inside) (pp.126-127)
9. Greene King Brewery Visitors' Centre (p.44)
10. Ornaments (p.23)
11. Dog and Partridge pub sign (p.110)
12. Westgate Brewery date (p.44)
13. Brewery chimneys (p.44)
14. Bridewell Lane School of Guildhall Foeffment (p.63)
15. Painted advert for Marlow's Builders' Supplies (p.85)
(in passing, note the grounds and buildings of the Sheltered accommodation in College Lane)
16. Beamed house and old shop front (p.40)
17. Ash Cottage (p.108)
18. Relief Pargetting (p.97)
19. 'Rose and Crown' with fine tile hanging (p.111)
20. St Edmund's RC Church (exterior and interior) (p.35)
Further on, across a major road junction is the 'Elephant and Castle pub sign (view without crossing main road) (p.110)